HOMELAND SECURITY

A CITIZEN'S GUIDE

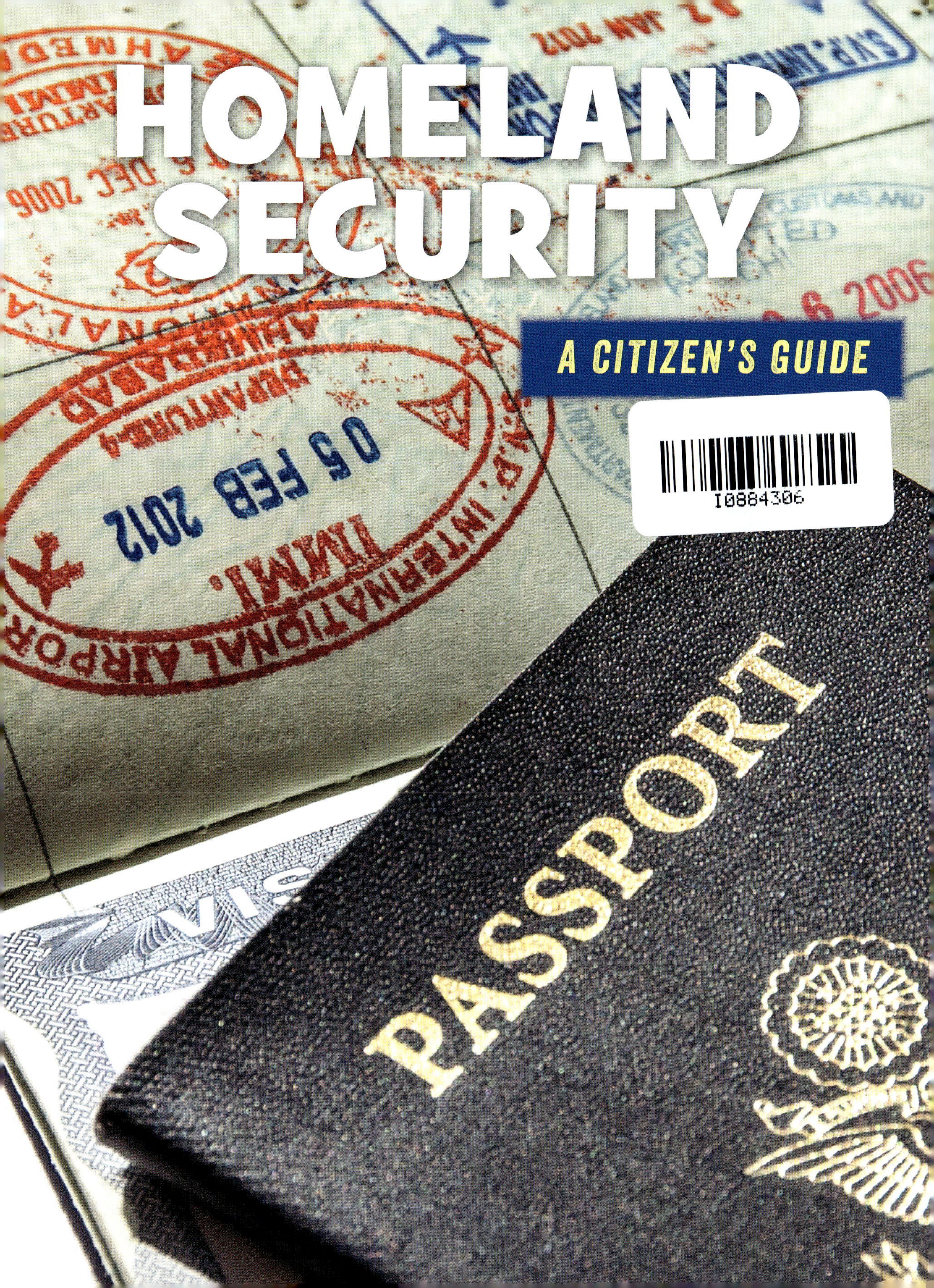

Published in the United States of America by Cherry Lake Publishing
Ann Arbor, Michigan
www.cherrylakepublishing.com

Content Adviser: Austin McCoy, Doctoral Candidate in History at the University of Michigan
Reading Adviser: Marla Conn MS, Ed., Literacy specialist, Read-Ability, Inc.

Photo Credits: © Kunal Mehta/Shutterstock, cover, 1; © Volt Collection/Shutterstock, 5; © Larry Bruce/Shutterstock, 6; © Christopher Halloran/Shutterstock, 8; © Photographee.eu/Shutterstock, 11; © StockLite/Shutterstock, 12; © Jaren Jai Wicklund/Shutterstock, 15; © Bart Everett/Shutterstock, 16; © Corepics VOF/Shutterstock, 18; © Anthony Correia/Shutterstock, 21; © J. Norman Reid/Shutterstock, 22; © Dragon Images/Shutterstock, 25; © Dusan Jankovic/Shutterstock, 26; © Arina P Habich/Shutterstock, 28

Library of Congress Cataloging-in-Publication Data
Names: Mara, Wil, author.
Title: Homeland security / Wil Mara.
Description: Ann Arbor : Cherry Lake Publishing, [2016] | Series: A citizen's guide | Includes bibliographical references and index.
Identifiers: LCCN 2016003905| ISBN 9781634710688 (hardcover) | ISBN 9781634711678 (pdf) | ISBN 9781634712668 (pbk.) | ISBN 9781634713658 (ebook)
Subjects: LCSH: United States. Department of Homeland Security—Juvenile literature. | National security—United States—Juvenile literature. | Civil defense—United States—Juvenile literature.
Classification: LCC HV6432.4 .M36 2016 | DDC 363.340973—dc23
LC record available at http://lccn.loc.gov/2016003905

Cherry Lake Publishing would like to acknowledge the work of the Partnership for 21st Century Learning. Please visit *www.p21.org* for more information.

Printed in the United States of America
Corporate Graphics

ABOUT THE AUTHOR

Wil Mara is an award-winning and best-selling author of more than 150 books, many of which are educational titles for young readers. Further information about his work can be found at www.wilmara.com.

TABLE OF CONTENTS

CHAPTER 1

What Is Homeland Security?

Have you ever been asked to take your shoes off in an airport security line? And then walk through a metal detector? And then watch while workers go through your backpack? These days, if you're flying to another city, you have to be ready for a few delays in getting to your plane. These safety measures were set up by the Transportation Security Administration (TSA), which is part of a new government body called the Department of Homeland Security (DHS). TSA agents work to make sure air travel remains as safe as possible for us. And they're just one part of the DHS.

The DHS is now the third-largest department in the United States government. The person who runs it, known as the secretary of homeland security, is a member of the president's cabinet. The cabinet is occupied by people the president trusts for

Airport security makes sure no one carries anything illegal onto a plane.

The 9/11 attacks forever changed how America addressed airport security.

honest and direct advice on all critical matters. They also include the vice president, the attorney general, and the secretaries of state, defense, and the treasury.

Congress created the DHS in November 2002. It combined 22 other agencies—a huge reorganization—plus it required some new positions as well. In the early days, the main thrust of the DHS was to more efficiently collect and analyze **data** from **intelligence**-gathering bodies. These included the Central Intelligence Agency (CIA), the Federal Bureau of Investigation (FBI), and the National Security Agency (NSA).

On September 11, 2001, the United States suffered the worst foreign attack on its soil since the bombing of Pearl Harbor by Japanese forces on December 7, 1941. A group of **terrorists** hijacked four commercial jets. Two were crashed into the World Trade Center towers in New York City, buildings that stood as symbols of American business and power. Another jet was flown into the Pentagon, the headquarters for the Department of Defense located in Arlington, Virginia. The fourth jet was on its way to Washington, D.C., when the passengers and crew, hearing

21st Century Content

Terrorism has unfortunately been around for hundreds of years. The basic definition of terrorism is the practice of using threats or violence to frighten or pressure others, often for making a statement against a political system. Religious and political groups and governments around the world have clashed since at least the first century. Even the famed Boston Tea Party, carried out by American rebels in 1773, was considered an act of terrorism. Nowadays extremists plan bombings and ***assassinations****. Today's terrorists have a startling array of tools at their disposal, including advanced weaponry, the funding and support of various governments, and the power of the Internet.*

George W. Bush was president from 2001 to 2009.

reports about the other three hijacked planes, physically fought with the terrorists to regain control of the plane. Experts believe the target was either the Capitol or the White House. Sadly, this plane crashed in a Pennsylvania cornfield, killing all on board. In total, about 3,000 innocent people perished on that tragic and horrifying day.

President George W. Bush decided that the United States needed to organize various groups within the government to work together to prevent further acts of terror. From this decision came the Department of Homeland Security, which had four main purposes. First, it would monitor all U.S. borders to prevent terrorists from entering. Second, it would help state and local authorities respond more quickly to terror-related incidents. Third, it would develop new technologies to detect weapons and protect citizens from their effects. And fourth, it would efficiently analyze intelligence from other government agencies to try and detect future attacks long before they occur.

CHAPTER 2

Gathering and Using Intelligence

A total of 19 men were involved in the four plane hijackings that took place on 9/11. Incredibly, American authorities came close to catching some of them before it happened. Two months before 9/11, an FBI agent in Phoenix, Arizona, wrote a note to his superiors at FBI headquarters in Washington, D.C. He suspected that a number of men taking flying lessons in Arizona belonged to a terrorist organization called **al-Qaeda**. He thought they might be planning to hijack airplanes. Around the same time, an FBI agent in Minnesota warned of a man in the United States who boasted that he could "fly something into the World Trade Center." And more than a decade earlier, the CIA had identified two other al-Qaeda members who were living overseas—but they didn't share this information with the FBI. Those two men

The FBI and CIA try to stop terrorists before they can carry out attacks.

eventually entered the United States and turned out to be two of the participants in the 9/11 attacks. It's likely the FBI would have kept a close watch on them if they'd known about them in the first place.

If the FBI and CIA had shared their data, the attacks might have been avoided. However, they had very different roles back then and rarely worked together. The FBI mainly focused on criminal activity within the United States, while the CIA followed suspicious activity outside the country. So neither group had any chance of seeing all the pieces of the puzzle.

The FBI and CIA send each other information on suspects.

It's the job of the DHS to make sure that this kind of "data disconnect" does not happen again. The DHS gathers information from the FBI, CIA, and numerous other agencies. Its intelligence specialists study the information. They figure out if terrorist activity is being planned. Then they post information on how likely the country is to experience a terrorist attack. The DHS keeps local and state law enforcement agencies informed about threats, and it aids the FBI in maintaining a list of known and suspected terrorists. This list is available to local, state, and federal authorities around the clock. If law enforcement officers get a tip or see something suspicious, they can quickly check for information on terrorists and suspects. Having critical data available at their fingertips helps officials fend off future attacks and ensure the safety of our citizens.

Life and Career Skills

Today, the Department of Homeland Security has more than 200,000 employees. They make use of all the latest technology to perform their jobs as efficiently as possible. They need to not only respond quickly when a **crisis** *arises, but also take steps to prevent crises from occurring in the first place. In order to succeed at this task, their most valuable asset is information. Sometimes it comes from the intelligence-gathering efforts of various government agencies. Other times, it comes from ordinary citizens who stay alert and report suspicious activity when they see it. What skills or personality traits do you think DHS workers have? Do you have of these skills or traits?*

CHAPTER 3

Protecting Borders and Airways

U.S. Customs officer Diana Dean was working at the border between Canada and the United States. Benni Noris was in the last car off the ferry in Port Angeles, Washington. He had just come from Victoria, British Columbia. When Dean asked Noris whom he was visiting, he replied that he was going to a hotel.

Dean felt something wasn't quite right. She had Noris pull over and open his trunk. U.S. Customs inspectors looked inside, and Noris took off running. Inspectors found materials for making bombs of massive power. Further, it turned out that Noris was not who he claimed—his real name was Ahmed Ressam. A little research by authorities revealed that he was a terrorist from Algeria. Noris was captured soon after and sent to prison.

Inspectors check cars that drive over the Canadian and Mexican borders into the United States.

This Coast Guard boat is patrolling near the Statue of Liberty, in New York City.

The DHS combined the U.S. Customs Service, Border Patrol, and parts of the former Immigration and Naturalization Service into a new entity called the Customs and Border Protection (CBP). The CBP and its officers are charged with big responsibilities. One of the borders they patrol is between the United States and Canada—which extends more than 5,000 miles (8,047 kilometers). They also monitor the dividing line between the United States and Mexico, which stretches nearly 2,000 miles (3,219 km). They have to remain **vigilant** around the clock because terrorists long ago determined the best times to try sneaking into the country.

Homeland Security also oversees the U.S. Coast Guard. The Coast Guard patrols the 95,000 miles (152,888 km) of U.S. shoreline, searching for not only terrorists but also smugglers, drug dealers, and other criminals. Together, the Coast Guard and the CBP inspect all shipping containers that enter the country. Thousands of these huge boxes arrive by boat every day. Patrol officers use handheld **chemical** and **radiation** detectors, plus giant x-ray machines. The technology is truly amazing, allowing officials to see straight through the walls of trucks and other vehicles that carry shipping containers. Inspectors can identify

Recently, many more jobs have opened up in the security industry.

chemical, **biological**, and **nuclear** material more easily than ever before.

The DHS also manages the Transportation Security Administration (TSA). Officers for this agency check luggage at hundreds of airports around the United States. The DHS also places undercover officers on planes to react in the event of terrorist activity. Since it is virtually impossible to detect one of these officers—often called a federal air marshal—on board, terrorists will have a much more difficult time carrying out future hijackings.

Life and Career Skills

Since the 9/11 tragedy, the security industry has grown by leaps and bounds, providing many career opportunities. Consider the job of inspecting every person and product entering the country. Hundreds of thousands of tons of cargo are shipped to the United States each year. In 2006, for example, CBP workers inspected 64,000 containers on trucks, trains, and ships. They also checked 365,000 passenger cars and trucks, and interviewed more than a million people entering the country every day! It's a lot of work—but it's a career that will provide safety and peace of mind for all Americans. What traits and qualities do you think you'd need in order to pursue such a job?

CHAPTER 4

Responding to Disasters

Emergency workers by the hundreds rushed to the World Trade Center in New York City on the morning of September 11, 2001. These incredibly brave men and women in the fire and police departments—often referred to as first responders—were not well-prepared to deal with the magnitude of the crisis they were facing. Fire chiefs on the scene sent orders via radio directly to the firefighters in the North and South Towers. The damage was widespread and severe. With so much chaos unfolding around them, it was difficult for the first responders to communicate efficiently. For example, the orders to evacuate the towers did not reach all the firefighters quickly enough, and many were killed when the towers collapsed. More than 400 rescue workers died that day in New York.

Hundreds of firefighters and police officers were injured or killed in the 9/11 attacks.

Homeland Security works with first responders around the country to prevent such losses in the future. The DHS gives specialized training directly to police departments, fire departments, and hospitals. It teaches them how to respond to all sorts of terroristic attacks, whether biological, chemical, or nuclear. The DHS also provides much of the necessary equipment to support these efforts.

Another important part of the DHS is the Federal Emergency Management Agency (FEMA). FEMA was originally created in 1979 to respond to tragic events and was put under the authority

Hurricane Katrina forced thousands of people out of their homes.

of Homeland Security in 2003. Through the years, FEMA has been on the scene immediately following devastating floods, tornadoes, hurricanes, wildfires, and other disasters. FEMA workers try to respond as quickly as possible, sometimes even helping citizens escape harm as the crisis is unfolding. It also provides support and comfort to victims after a crisis. For example, FEMA sent five search-and-rescue teams to the Pentagon after the 9/11 attacks. Twenty more teams went to the World Trade Center to help find victims and recover the bodies of those who had perished.

21st Century Content

FEMA's work does not always go smoothly. Following the devastating effects of Hurricane Katrina when it struck New Orleans, Louisiana, on August 29, 2005, thousands of residents became homeless. FEMA workers brought people food, water, blankets, clothing, medicine, and more. But their response efforts were poorly planned in many ways. Sports stadiums and government buildings were filled with people displaced from their homes, and FEMA was unprepared to deal with the needs of so many. Criticism also fell on the DHS for not doing more in advance of the disaster, particularly since the National Hurricane Center had predicted Katrina's force and effect two days beforehand. Since then, DHS has made numerous changes to its response planning. It has created hurricane-management teams, trained its employees to handle a wide variety of worst-case scenarios, and upgraded much of its equipment.

CHAPTER 5

The Right to Privacy?

As a result of the 9/11 attacks, the U.S. government focused on improving security around the nation. The Department of Homeland Security was one result of that effort. Another was that security agencies were given power to undertake various activities for the sake of protecting American citizens. For example, Congress passed laws to improve the security of air travel. The airplane doors that separate the pilots from the passengers are now lockable and reinforced so they are nearly impossible to break down. Also, pilots are allowed to carry guns if they wish and are trained by the TSA to use them properly. And airport security is now handled by government officials instead of private security firms.

The PATRIOT Act allowed the NSA to collect a lot of phone data from American citizens.

Security improvements like these are clearly good for all citizens. But not all measures taken by the DHS have been celebrated by the public. Following the 9/11 attacks, the U.S. government was granted legal power to explore private areas of people's lives more deeply than ever before. This gave rise to the question, "How much is too much?"

One of the most controversial new laws was the USA PATRIOT Act, which was passed in October 2001. It expanded the FBI's ability to conduct **surveillance**, making it easier for FBI agents to get permission to listen to people's conversations.

Under the PATRIOT Act, the FBI has more power to monitor people's email accounts.

They could also track someone's e-mail and Internet usage more easily, and acquire a person's medical and financial records.

Many people believe spying on people violates their **civil liberties**. In the United States, citizens are allowed to think and say what they feel without fear of punishment. The right to privacy and free speech is a privilege guaranteed by the Constitution. Other civil liberties are at stake, too. For example, there have been numerous cases of ethnic profiling by FBI agents and airport security officials since the 9/11 attacks. The hijackers were from Saudi Arabia and other countries in the

Middle East. And al-Qaeda is a terrorist organization rooted in the Middle East. But some people have been held and searched at airports for no other reason than because they appeared to be from the Middle East. Is singling out people simply because of their appearance taking security too far?

This leads us to a challenging question. How far should we allow our freedoms to be restricted for the sake of security? Some say that the danger from terrorism is so great that the government should have even more power to invade people's

21st Century Content

The president's relationship with other countries varies from warm and friendly to distant and prickly. Countries that have been longtime friends and stood by the United States in difficult times will rarely be a problem for the president. Those that have posed greater challenges, however, have to be handled with careful diplomacy. Generally, the president often leaves it to members of his cabinet to deal with unfriendly nations. The president may dictate the policy, but someone like the secretary of state will be the one who communicates with the leadership of those nations.

The Department of Homeland Security tries to keep everyone safe.

privacy, in order to gain intelligence. Others say too much power in this regard is a dire threat to the fundamental principles upon which America is based. Civil rights and liberties are guaranteed in the Constitution, which forms the very basis of the nation. So how do we strike that perfect balance? It isn't only up to the Department of Homeland Security to figure this out—it's up to all of us. Working together, we should, in time, be able to find that balance and enjoy our rights while protecting and preserving our lives.

21st Century Content

Not all terrorists come from other countries. Some were born and raised right here in America. One was Timothy McVeigh, born in New York in 1968. On April 19, 1995, McVeigh parked a rented truck loaded with explosives outside the Alfred P. Murrah Federal Building in Oklahoma City, Oklahoma. People were just getting to work and leaving their children at a day care center on the first floor. At 9:02 a.m., the truck blew up and destroyed half the building. The blast killed 168 people and injured more than 500 others. It was the worst act of terrorism on U.S. soil up to that point.

Think About It

Watching the news can be really scary these days! It's important to be aware of problems in the world, but remember that most of these things are probably far away from where you live. If you ever get upset hearing about terrorism, talk to your parents about it. They can answer questions you might have. If you have a friend or sibling who gets upset by the news, what could you do to make him or her feel better?

How and when did your family come to the United States? See if you can get some stories from your parents. Did they immigrate here (together or separately)? Were your grandparents the first ones to come? Or has your family been here even longer than that? Draw a diagram with a map and a family tree, and talk about it with a classmate.

Reread Chapter 5, about the government's monitoring of phone and email. How do you feel about this? Do you think the extra safety is worth the invasion of privacy? How would you feel if you found out you or your family were being monitored?

For More Information

BOOKS

Green, Robert. *Terrorism*. Ann Arbor, MI: Cherry Lake Publishing, 2008.

McCabe, Matthew. *12 Things to Know About Terrorism*. Mankato, MN: 12-Story Library, 2014.

Mullins, Matt. *Homeland Security*. Ann Arbor, MI: Cherry Lake Publishing, 2010.

ON THE WEB

FEMA—Ready: Be a Hero!
www.ready.gov/kids

KidsHealth—Terrorism
http://kidshealth.org/en/kids/terrorist-attacks.html

U.S. Department of Homeland Security
www.dhs.gov

GLOSSARY

al-Qaeda (al-KYE-duh) a militant organization founded in the late 1980s whose members are Muslims with extreme views

assassinations (uh-SAS-uh-NAY-shuns) the murders of people who are well-known or important

biological (bye-uh-LAH-jih-kuhl) relating to the study of life and all living things

chemical (KEM-i-kuhl) of or having to do with chemistry or chemicals

civil liberties (SIV-uhl LIB-ur-teez) people's rights to do or say things that are not illegal without being stopped or interrupted by the government

crisis (KRYE-sis) a time of severe difficulty or danger

data (DAY-tuh) information collected in a place so that something can be done with it

intelligence (in-TEL-ih-juhns) information about what is happening or is going to happen, especially when obtained by spying

nuclear (NOO-klee-ur) of or having to do with the energy created by splitting atoms

radiation (ray-dee-AY-shuhn) atomic particles that are sent out from a radioactive substance

surveillance (sir-VAY-luns) close watch kept over someone or something

terrorists (TER-ur-ists) people who use violence and threats in order to frighten people, obtain political power, or force a government to do something

vigilant (VIJ-uh-luhnt) keeping a careful watch

INDEX